Prayers & Litanies

for the Christian Seasons

Prayers & Litanies

for the Christian Seasons

Sharlande Sledge

SMYTH&HELWYS
PUBLISHING, INCORPORATED • MACON, GEORGIA

Smyth & Helwys Publishing, Inc.
6316 Peake Road
Macon, Georgia 31210-3960
1-800-747-3016
©1999 by Smyth & Helwys Publishing
All right reserved.
Printed in the United States of America.

Sharlande Sledge

The paper used in this publication meets the minimum requirements of
American National Standard for Information Sciences—Permanence of
Paper for Printed Library Materials.
ANSI Z39.48–1984. (alk. paper)

Library of Congress Cataloging-in-Publication Data

Sledge, Sharlande, 1952–
        Prayers and litanies for the Christian seasons/
        Sharlande Sledge.
        pp.   cm.
        ISBN 1-57312-192-4 (alk. paper)
        1. Church year—Prayerbooks and devotions—English.
        2. Baptists—Prayerbooks and devotions—English.
        3. Litanies—Baptists.
        4. Pastoral prayers.
        I. Title.
        BV30.S55 1999
        264'.061013—dc21   98-37031
                                                        CIP

ISBN 1-573132-192-4

With love and gratitude
for my friends and family
at Lake Shore Baptist Church

Contents

Lent

Foreword

"Words and WORD . . . among the many, let us hear the ONE" is a public prayer of illumination I have used for years prior to preaching. The intent of the prayer is to ask God to help us be found by the Living Word of Christ amidst the plethora of human words used in worship, especially in the preaching event. My former colleague in ministry, Sharlande Sledge, took this prayer as a guiding principle in her life, the result of which is this superb book of pulpit prayers.

Sharlande is an artisan with words. She understands the power of language. She knows that words can explode into our imagination and send us into places of human misery intent on making a creative response to suffering. She understands the strength of words to heal wounds or surface lingering resentments that dissipate in their telling. She lives with a constant fascination about the stories we all carry within our souls, stories requiring words to bring them to fullness. The crafting of words, then, is an active calling for her, a potent means to explore this faith that prophesies and consoles, challenges and for-gives, demands and sustains.

The highest understanding of all for Sharlande Sledge is that in the Mystery of God, the Living Word of Christ is set free within the constraints of our human language, and that is miracle, indeed. When a word of forgiveness is spoken, it is the Living Christ who speaks blessing and bears away the burden. When a word of hope is shared, it is the Living Christ who lifts spirits and crushes despair. When a word of demand is pronounced, it is the Living Christ who brings vision and sends feet marching. Sharlande knows that among the many, many human words always exists the possibility that the Living Word of Christ will spring forth and kingdom opportunities will abound.

In his classic work on prayer, *The Soul of Prayer*, British theologian and pastor P. T. Forsyth wrote: "Prayer is the highest use to which speech can be put. It is the highest meaning that can be put into words. Indeed, it breaks through language and escapes into action." In a prayer entitled "Imagine," Sharlande Sledge demonstrates Forsyth's conviction. Calling on the hearer to allow their view of the world to be transformed, she writes:

> Through our imagination,
> shape our perception.
> Take us places we have never been.
> Loosen the grip of our eyes
> that stare transfixed at old patterns.
> Free us to be surprised, confused, amazed
> by the undreamed-of ways
> you choose to be revealed to us.

Such prayers burst into the "stuck" places of our living and dislodge old standards of faith until our encounters with the Living Christ become fresh again. I commend these prayers to you as vehicles that will transport you to new places on the journey of faith. Pray them and be changed.

—Roger A. Paynter
Senior Pastor
First Baptist Church
Austin, Texas

Acknowledgments

My parents—Margaret and Rupert Sledge surrounded me with books and love, making it easy for me to lose myself in the mystery of both "words" and "Word" at an early age.

My pastors—Welton Gaddy was the pastor of Broadway Baptist Church, Fort Worth, Texas, where I celebrated Advent for the first time and learned so much about the sacredness of congregational worship. I have served with three pastors at Lake Shore Baptist Church in Waco, Texas. Roger Paynter's compassionate and prophetic preaching changed the way I heard the good news and gave me the push I needed toward the pulpit. Nathan Stone affirmed my leanings toward pastoral care and prayer. Brett Younger, my colleague in ministry today, has been as excited about this book as I have, and has been an invaluable source of help with theological questions that have come to me day in and day out while writing.

The people of Lake Shore Baptist Church—They have heard my prayers and sometimes graciously asked for copies of them. Joan Rectenwald, in particular, encouraged me for years to publish them. Gary Miller and Catherine Davenport, my coaches in computer literacy, helped get the manuscript from laptop to paper.

Judy Prather—My creative friend is as amazed by the beauty and power of words as I am. She has joined me in the search for "the right word" to offer in worship so many times. From the afternoon the idea for this book was first conceived, she has kept the dream alive and nudged it into being.

June Osborne—My splendid, devoted friend has spent long and good hours poring over each word of each revision with me, making detailed editorial suggestions. For her spiritual guidance, which constantly teaches me that "everything has meaning" and sometimes "no words are necessary," my gratitude knows no end.

Preface

Each year on the Saturday before Advent the worship committee members at Lake Shore Baptist Church hang elegant velvet banners high on the walls of the sanctuary, reminders of past Advent seasons celebrated at our church. I always ask them to hang my favorite banner where I can see it during worship on Sunday mornings. It is rich dark burgundy with forest green letters. The words on the banner are the essence of Advent for me: "words & Word . . . among the many, the One."

The theme was inspired by a prayer my friend and former pastor, Roger Paynter, created one morning here at Lake Shore. It speaks "to the idea that the reality of our existence is tied up in words that are plentiful and powerful." We live by words—good words, healing words, strong words, redemptive words, holy words. But, human beings that we are, we also speak and live words that are noisy and oppressive, words that hurt, clutter, divide, abuse, and exhaust.

The "in the beginning" Word became flesh and dwelled among us, so we might live into the words that bring wholeness, healing, justice, comfort, and love. In the powerful Word of Jesus Christ, words such as "compassion" and "presence" and "resurrection" are defined in their fullest sense. Try as we might, we cannot completely express the meanings of the words. Yet in our earthbound language we still attempt to catch hold of the meanings God intended. Our hearts want to respond to the Living Word, so we create words and sentences and stories, prayers and poems and hymns to offer God.

I am awestruck by words—the way the letters curl onto each other in calligraphy; the way my ear hears them differently when they are whispered, shouted, spoken, or sung; how their meaning is shaped by my faith and how my faith is shaped by their meaning. I could carry "grace" and "extravagance" and "homecoming" around in my pockets, knowing I could take them out at any time, turn them over like smooth stones, and be blessed by their memory and meaning.

I also know that "pain," "hunger," "sacrifice," and "darkness" are part of the vocabulary of faith. In ways we will never fully comprehend with human understanding, they are transformed by the One Word that empowers all other words. Mysteriously, the words that describe our deepest longings for God and our most distant wanderings from God are often the starting points of our prayers.

Each prayer in this collection is focused on a word that has, indeed, been a starting point for a prayer. I have offered each of them in public worship at Lake Shore Baptist Church in Waco, Texas, my congregation since 1985. Many were first voiced as pastoral prayers; others were invocations or litanies of praise. The people's needs and joys during the week pointed me toward a prayerful word for Sunday.

This book takes you through the seasons of the church year—Advent, Christmas, Epiphany, Lent, Easter, and Pentecost. The words are arranged alphabetically within each season. Some words fall naturally into the cycle of the seasons—for example, "preparation" is an Advent word, just as "brokenness" is a Lenten word, and "church," a Pentecost word. But our needs as praying people are not bound by calendar pages. Dip into the book at any time, any place. Look in the index to find a word. Use the prayers on the title pages for each season as invocations. Borrow a line here or there. Turn what was composed as a prayer for the people into a litany, or a litany into a benediction. Read them silently or out loud with your congregation.

As our spirits search for God, they will encounter a world of words. "words and Word, O God" . . . among the many, may we each meet the One.

Advent

Come, Emmanuel God, in whatever way you will.
Be Light that guides us
trembling toward the manger,
dazzles us into irrational love,
and shines hope into the world's forgotten places.
Little by little, give us Light in its completeness
until at last we see you face to face.
O come, O come, Emmanuel.

Awakening

Wake us up, God!

Here we are,
rubbing the sleep out of our eyes,
still drowsy and dozing.
And you, Emmanuel God,
are awake with life,
coming to us from on high
to startle us with incarnation.

Stretching and yawning
from ordinary time,
we stumble to the door of your Advent.
At first we may not recognize
the outline of your face.
The night is too much with us,
but the dawning is with you.
The light whispers your coming.

So wake us up, Lord Jesus.
Wake us when our expectations are too low.
Wake us when our expectations are too high.
Wake us when we least expect it.
Wake us to your everlasting light.

Coming

Come to us, Lord Jesus,
in every purple-patterned life,
every wrap of loving arms
in shivering December.

Come to us in the midst of our preparations,
in spite of our preparations.

Come, Lord Jesus,
not just to those we can see
in this warm, comfortable place,
but come to all your children.

Come to your children
in places where the land is
parched with drought
or cracked with ice,
where lines are drawn
with terrifying precision
between one ethnic group and another,
between those whose hands have the power
to open bags of grain
and those whose hands hold nothing.

In your spirit of healing and wholeness,
redeem and transform our world.

Come to your children whose cries
echo through the darkness for you.
Come to open the ears of our hearts,
so that we can hear your morning call.
Come to shake us awake and nudge us to the dawn,
so we may shine reflections of your light.

Come by here . . . and there . . . and there.
"O come, O come, Emmanuel."

Darkness

God of heaven and earth,
in this drama of Advent and Christmas,
our lines do not follow the expected script.
Some of us are hurting from the inside out
as much as others are celebrating their joy.
Amid talk about fulfillment,
loss looms large.

Remind us that you come to us
as the Incarnate Christ
whether we have mustered
the strength to light a candle
or decided to sit in darkness.
You reach out to us
whether we are singing jubilantly
or weeping uncontrollably.

We wait for you to come to us
where we are,
as we are—
numb,
grieving,
fragile,
coping,
out-of-sync with the season's songs.

Punch a hole in the darkness
that swallows us
to let in a glimmer of hope.

Sometimes a pinprick of light
is all we need.

Expectation

Will you come to our world, God?
Will you come with hope?
For we have too many good intentions,
not enough hopes realized;
too many questions, too little assurance;
too many longings, too few prayers.
O come, O come, Emmanuel. When you come, bring hope.

Will you come to our world, God?
Will you come with peace?
For we have too much brokenness,
not enough wholeness;
too much frantic activity, not enough calm;
too many worries, not enough dreams.
O come, O come, Emmanuel. When you come, bring peace.

Will you come to our world, God?
Will you come with joy?
For we have too much seriousness,
not enough laughter;
too many expectations, not enough celebration;
too many words, too little singing.
O come, O come, Emmanuel. When you come, bring joy.

Will you come to our world, God?
Will you come with love?
For we have too much loneliness,
not enough friendship;
too many rules, not enough gospel;
too much getting, not enough caring.
O Come, O come, Emmanuel. When you come, bring love.

Come, Bringer of Hope.
Come, Prince of Peace.
Come, Giver of Joy.
Come, Lover of All People. Come, O Come, Emmanuel.

Imagine

Imagining God,
immerse us in the fullness of your world
so that we are up to our hearts in colors
and up to our ears in love.

Help us take a second look
at those around us
to notice your presence
in each person we meet.
Through our imagination,
shape our perceptions.
Take us places we have never been.
Loosen the grip of our eyes
that stare transfixed at old patterns.
Free us to be surprised, confused, amazed
by the undreamed-of ways
you choose to be revealed to us.
Allow us to participate
in your imagination,
to see ourselves, our neighbors, and our world
full of possibility and promise,
ready to be transformed.

When we feel that our lives are like
a box full of puzzle pieces tossed on the table,
in faith, help us imagine ourselves whole.

When the news brings an image of evil,
in faith, help us imagine a world
where hurting people can ask for help
and receive it from a caring community.

When our courage fails
and we need someone
to hold us up or calm us down,
in faith, help us imagine a church
where we can do things together
that we cannot do alone.

When we are called
into relationship with the world
but feel consumed
by what is two feet in front of us,
in faith, help us imagine
you in the eyes of each person we see.

With you,
let us imagine the world at peace.
With you,
let us imagine our purpose
at one with yours.
Oh, God,
let all our imaginings
be not merely dreams
but the beginning of our moving
in the world with you.

Imagine with us, God.
Imagine.
Imagine.

Preparation

Wake up, people of God!
The Word of God is coming to dwell among us.

World, watch! Do not sleep!
For the realm of God is near.

Prepare for the unexpected to break into your lives;
be alert to the signs of the coming of God.

But we are exiles in a strange land,
hoping for news of a Savior to help us.

Look for the Light that was with God in the beginning.
Even while you are seeking your home,
prepare a dwelling place for the Lord.

We will wait without fully knowing;
we will rest in the stillness
with the company of faith, hope, and love.

Wake up, people of God! Look for the Light!
Listen attentively for the coming of the Word.

Out of our silent night or our midnight clear
with all the heavens and earth, we will sing "Joy to the World."

The Lord is coming to bring us peace.

Sing "*Noel.*"

Sing "*gloria in excelsis deo.*"

Risk

Risktaker God,
help us empty our hearts
to make room for the birth
of something new
and altogether unforeseen.

Cast off the shadows of whatever
we assume will sustain us,
so we can receive the light
of the unknown things
you have in store.

When we are full of our own ideas,
there is no room for the birth of hope.
When you are looking for a warm room for a baby,
we are inside our homes with the doors closed.

During Advent may we accept your invitation
to come out of our safe places—
to let go, to open up—
not to forsake the things and people we treasure
but to learn to hold them lightly and freely.

What do you have in store for us, God?
While we are preparing a home for you,
what are you preparing for us?
What is taking up too much room in our hearts?

O, God, assure us it is all right
if we do not have all the answers
because that is what Advent is all about . . .
waiting without knowing,
waiting with nothing but faith, hope, and love
in the company of God's love,
a love that promises everything,
even your advent,
to those who have saved you room.

Wait

We wait for peace to come to all hearts and all nations,
but we are reluctant to let our vision of the world be changed.

We wait for love to be born afresh in the world each day,
**but we forget that the light we reflect in our words and actions
is how the Light of Advent shines in the world.**

We wait for Christ to be born again this season,
**but we confess that we find the coming birth
yet another event in our crowded lives.**

We wait with the dream of getting our tasks accomplished
once and for all,
but we catch ourselves in the mode of "hurry up and wait."

We wait, listening to the familiar songs and stories of the season,
**but we leave no room for the surprising newness
of the prophets' expectation.**

We want to wait with the anticipation of children,
**but we are far too "grown up" to love
without calculating the cost of your friendship.**

We wait to be the people God intended us to be,
but we forget that the grace of our becoming is a gift of God.

We wait with hope in the darkness
and focus our eyes upon the one small glimmer of light,
for in it we shall see the salvation of the Lord.

And we shall wait no longer.

Word

O God, you are the Word among all words
that spoke words into being.

But you did not remain a distant word,
speaking only in the language
of darkness and light,
day and night,
sea and stars.

You came to live among us,
talking in the everyday language of
all who need a word of forgiveness,
all who long for a word of love,
all who pray for a word of hope.

And now we dare to speak to you
in words of our creation.
Take our words and live your grace through them.
Transform our words, and change our lives through them.

And when our words are too deep to speak aloud,
we pray that your Spirit will speak them for us
so that all the words of our mouths
and the meditations of our hearts
will be acceptable in your sight,
the Word beyond all words.

Christmas

*Word among all words,
dwell among us.
Very God of very God,
live in our world for a while.
Vulnerable Child,
be our God in human flesh.
Holy Babe of Bethlehem,
cry our tears with us.
Eternity captured in human time,
reveal your glory to the nations.
Word made flesh,
live, breathe, walk among us.*

Adoration

Holy Love born in a manger,
bathed in the light of the star,
we pause to whisper our worship before you.

Creator of all that was and is and yet shall be,
the universe reverberates with joy,
and our voices echo its "glorias."

Deity perfectly expressed in human flesh,
Dayspring from on high,
you breathe peace on our earthly hearts.

Thirsting babe,
born for the hunger of the world,
we listen to your infant cries.

Mystery made visible,
loved into Light,
we may soon leap and dance our joy
or one day build a cathedral to the heavens in your name.

But tonight, in quietness and stillness,
we keep watch before your cradle.

Blessing

Go into this new year to be a beginning for others—

**to be a singer to the songless,
a storyteller to the wanderer;**

to become a beginning of hope for the despairing,
of healing for the hurting,

**of assurance for the doubting,
of reconciliation for the divided.**

Go forth believing in beginnings,
making beginnings, being beginnings

**so that you may not just grow old
but grow new each day of this amazing life
God calls us to live with each other.**

In the name of the God of ages past,
who makes all things new,

**so we can remember yesterday,
dream of tomorrow,**

and live in God's love today.

Go in the peace of Christ.

Christ Child

Newborn God,
you are as young as an infant child,
yet ageless as the oceans, mountains, and stars.
Two thousand years have not
diminished your presence.
Indeed, you add splendor to splendor,
and the intensity of your face shines brighter still
for those who recognize your presence.

Enter every longing heart.
Awaken our eyes, God,
as you did Simeon's old and cloudy ones.
Shine your incomprehensible,
in-the-beginning presence
through the sunlight and into our hearts
so that we can see beyond the poverty of Mary and Joseph
to the treasure of the child Jesus.

We long to see the Word made flesh,
for we, like Simeon and Anna,
are a mixture of fragile hope and aging bodies.

Let us learn from them and all the wise ones
who guide us in faith
that you are the one for whom we have been waiting;
that your grace is lived out in gladness, shared sorrow,
and eternal tenderness among us;
that your face is fleshed out again and again
in all your children;
and that your blessing is upon us,
for in you our eyes have seen the glory of the Lord.

Expectancy

Wondrous Worker of Wonders,
we praise you not only for what has been
or for what is, but for what is yet to be,
for you are gracious beyond all telling of it.

We praise you that out of the turbulence of life
a kingdom is coming,
is being shaped even now
out of our bits of trusting
and sprigs of hoping
and seeds of caring.

Teach us to expect a message from angels,
a redeemer from a baby in a manger,
gifts from hidden places,
your kingdom born amid ordinary folk like us.

How silently,
how silently,
your wondrous gifts are given.

We would be silent now, Lord,
and expectant
that we may receive
the gifts we need,
so we may become
the gifts others need.

Fulfillment

O, Lord, you have come!

You have broken through the darkness of our world,
and so we sing your praise.

You introduced joy to our world—
joy that outlasts the festivities of December
joy that supersedes the excited activity of Christmas Day,
joy that comes to us and remains with us
because of your abiding love.

In an act of love,
you closed the circle between
promise and fulfillment
Creator and created
Word and world.

We worship the Christ who grew up
to show us what God is like,
who called all people unto him
and who calls us
to share the Incarnate Word with the world.

So as a church now we sing:
"Come and worship, come and worship.
Worship Christ the newborn King"

Gifts

Glorious God,
like the sudden brilliance of the star
shining into sleepy shepherds' eyes,
you bring us surprising light in the darkness.

How do we capture the song of the angels?
How do we count all the stars in the sky?
How do we measure your great love for us?

Like Mary, we ponder in our hearts all
we have seen and heard,
and we cannot keep our joy to ourselves.

May our gifts be flashes of brightness
sent into all the world
in the name of Christ
who is our Light
and the sign unto us
of God's redeeming love.

Incarnation

Emmanuel God,
We are here tonight looking for incarnation.
We come to cradle the holy in our arms,
to hear the newborn cry of the divine creator,
to see you decked out in flesh.
We gather around the manger
as midwives to your birth.
We're here for the ceremony
of giving you a human name.

We're here for a closer glimpse at mystery
. . . if that can be.
and a brush with the presence of angels
. . . if that can be.
and a glimpse of the star of all stars
. . . if that can be.

We have need of such things, God—
all that is brilliant and wondrous and
unexpectedly bright,
all that merges mystery with the manger.

But we have more need of your presence
that is with us always.
Come again, Emmanuel God,
to dwell among us.
Bring us your grace and truth.

Joy

Come, Lord Jesus,
and bring joy to our world.

Joy to the worshiper
who has sung the carols for seventy seasons
and still sings them with heart and soul and voice.

Joy to the child
looking at the flickering candles
who knows we are celebrating
something too mysterious to explain in words.

Joy to the one who needs to know
that though your love encompasses the whole world,
it is particular enough to meet each grief and loss
as though it were the only pain in the world.

Joy to the homeless mother
who longs to carry with her
the assurance of your being at home
with those the world tosses aside.

Joy to all of us
caught up in the wonders of your love
as though we were experiencing your birth
for the first time.

With all heaven and nature,
let us sing
and shout
and speak
our joy to the world!

Rejoice

"Good Christian friends, rejoice!
With heart and soul and voice!"
Break forth into singing
for God has visited and comforted God's people.

**The Christmas season continues,
and the spirit of Christ reigns among us.**

Our hearts rejoice
because the sins and sorrows of this world
crumble under the wonders of God's love.

**Our souls rejoice
because the One by whom and for whom all things exist
welcomes us as brothers and sisters of Jesus Christ.**

Our voices rejoice
because the Word became flesh and dwelled among us,
full of grace and truth.

**With heart and soul and voice,
we rejoice that the Word was Light and Life to all,
and the darkness has not overcome it.**

Thanks to our light-bringing, life-giving God!

Epiphany

Creator of the stars of light, break into our world.
God of surprising love, made manifest in Jesus Christ,
call us to courage, vision, and change.
From north, south, east, and west,
we arise to follow your light.

Attention

Creator of the most delicate eggshell and the most brilliant butterfly,
you let each seed drop through your fingers to flower the earth
and painted every feather with the finest strokes of your brush.
You filled the earth with stones and seashells and herbs
and pine cones by the billions, each a wonder of design.
Your attention to detail in nature astounds us.

And yet you care most of all for your children.
The particularity of your love amazes us.
You would turn over a rock to find us.
You would search for us like a child looking for a four-leaf clover.
You delight in our presence, just as we are delighted
when we see daffodils poking through the cold February earth.

You love each of us without measure.
And you hurt with each of us without measure.
O, Creator God, may those who are hurting
know the grace of your healing love
in the particular ways that give them strength.
Only you fully know their needs.
So we trust that you will hold each one in your hands
as gently as you held them as children
and let them rest in your arms.

Give each one a glimpse of light even in the night of deepest pain.
Give each one the touch that calms and reassures.
Give each one a memory every day to bring joy.
Give each one a word of strength and hope.

O, God, we cannot give all these things like you can,
but each day we can offer one particular thing to one person.
However you see fit, use us as bearers of your grace
to the one we see right in front of us
and, through prayer, to those who are miles away.

Baptism

We gather to witness the story of God's salvation
acted out in the waters of baptism.
In holy worship, remember your baptism,
and give thanks.

**As we watch the picture of putting away old things
and rising to walk in newness of life,
once again we hear Jesus Christ call us
to live into the risky vocation
of Christian discipleship.**

Through our baptism we are marked as a peculiar people
who believe in the radical act
of our redemption through Jesus Christ.

**We are immersed into newness of life
and raised to walk on mission
with Christ in the world.**

We do not know what new thing will be born in us,
but we ask God's grace to respond in Christlike love.

**Let us listen once again for the voice from heaven,
naming us the beloved children of God,
connecting us to all who have felt the waters of baptism
soaking them in grace.**

God, drench us in the living water of your love.
Immerse us in the depths of life in your Spirit.

Raise us once again to walk in new life with you.

Calling

God, it's a tall order you set before us—
to be light to the world.
Do you really think we're up to it?

Are we the kind of people you envision
going home from the manger a different way?
Did you have in mind such fearful folk
to minister alongside you,
people like us who forget to carry our light
any farther than our doorsteps?

And the world as our place of service?
God, our candles are already burning at both ends.
Sometimes your holy calling is an idea
too big to get our hearts around.

But the more we know of you, the more we know that
you imagine us as your fellow servants on the road
and that it is through us that your light shines into the world.

Thanks to you for the daily challenge and blessing of
giving back a portion of what you graciously give us,
experiencing your mercy and blessing,
mourning the suffering of a broken world,
celebrating the promise of a liberating gospel,
moving into the frozen places of the world with warmth
and into the parched places with water.

Help us take the risk of exposing our hearts,
finding the lost,
healing the broken,
feeding the hungry,
releasing the prisoners,
rebuilding the nations,
bringing peace among the people,
starting here where we have known you
who knows us so well.

Faith

God of life,
God of all our becoming
winding
changing
hopeful
fearful years—
we praise you
for your faithfulness.
When we look back
through all our
deciding
planning
wishing
through doors closed
through windows opened
through best-laid plans
and worst-kept secrets,
how can we deny your providence and grace
at work in the fabric of our lives?
Even allowing for our great gifts
of rationalization
and special pleading,
how can we look back
and not see
haunting traces of your grace?
Why can we not see that your hand
is present and is moving over things to come?
We ask no road map
no guarantees
no inoculation against human life.
But when we are hurting
and pain floods our vision,
grant us faith to cry our tears.
When we are strong,
grant us faith willing to be surprised.
God of all our becoming, we praise you.

Home

O Lord, you have always been our home.
From everlasting to everlasting,
you have been our refuge and our strength,
our dwelling place for all generations.

O Lord, you are the home toward which our ancestors traveled.

You are the sanctuary that called them from all things familiar
toward the promise of a new country.
Through stars and clouds and faithful attention to dreams,
you guided them through the desert to the oasis of your love.

**O Lord, you are the home we know in Jesus Christ
who came to dwell among us.**

You inhabit the very earth on which we live.
With open arms of hospitality you invite us into your presence.
You heal our wounds. You call us to the table, and extend our vision
to see others who need your welcome.

O Lord, you are the home we know in the Spirit who guides us.

You are the memory of where we have been
and the anticipation of where we are going.
Though we are not yet in possession of all we have been promised,
here and there along the way we catch glimpses of our eternal home.

**O Lord, you are our home along the way
and at the end of our journey.**

For traveling with us,
for rescuing us when we are lost,
and for calling us into your holy place,
thanks be to you, O God, our eternal home.

Hope

Come, Lord Jesus.
Come into our world.
Come . . . to soften our fear
and untangle the knots of our anxiety.
Come . . . to quiet our trembling
and gentle our desperation.
Come . . . to wipe the tears from our eyes
and ease the pains in the bodies and souls
of those we love.
Come . . . to gather the broken handfuls of
our spirits and shape them into a stronger whole.
Come . . . to give us the assurance we know
in the approach of a friend we long to see.
Come . . . to resurrect our perspective
when we are disappointed.
Come . . . to deepen our hurt
until we learn to share it.
Come . . . to pry us off dead center
until we are moved to tears
or work or smiles or dreams.
Come . . . to steady us
as we tremble in our "maybe's."
Come with us toward what counts
but can only be measured in
bread shared,
bodies healed,
spirits lifted,
water poured,
light in the darkness,
joy in the morning,
company for the lonely,
quiet for the frenzied,
your name being praised,
and our becoming a chorus calling
"Come, Lord Jesus."

Journey

Where are you, pilgrims? Do you know?

Once we were in familiar territory.
But now God has called us out
and away from home.
We do not know where God is leading.
We often wander about in our own land
without bread, a roof, a map.
And without a guide,
we are not sure where to go.

Do you see the Light?
Do you see it beckoning you forward,
calling you away and home again?
It is the Light of God, shining for you.

Journeying God, pitch your tent with us,
so that we may not become deterred
by unfamiliar landscapes
and detours in the road.

At every turn we are blessed and contained
by your ancient and steadfast love
that continually and insistently sustains us.

Through your Word,
give us strength to continue our pilgrimage,
searching for your Light to guide the way.

Love

Love that will not let us go,
we rest our weary souls in thee.

This week some of us have traced
rainbows through the rain
and finally looked up to see
the colors shining after the storm.
Others are still longing for
signs of hope to be made real to them.

Loving God,
hear our prayers for those
who need the sound of your love
spoken clearly into their winter-weary souls.
Too many days our attention has settled
on ourselves instead of focusing
on your invitations to love others.
May our response to your love be love.

With our whole hearts,
let us spend our love with abandon
and risk our love with no thought for our own gain
so that our neighbors will know your caring love,
the hurting will know your healing love,
and those whom we say we love
will know that indeed we do.

Nations

God of all nations,
Your Spirit transcends the boundaries of geography and time.

If we travel to African villages parched by drought
and frightened by violence, you are there.
If we journey to Middle Eastern countries caught in the clash
of religions and cultures, you are there.
If we make our home in Latin American cities separated from
us more by economics than by distance, you are there.
If we move to places in our country far from
the comfort of family and friends, you are there.

God, you are where we cannot be at this hour
except through our prayers . . .
with the Bosnian mother crying in the night for her children
with the Bedouin shepherd rising with the sun
with the elderly American facing a weekend of loneliness.

As today becomes tomorrow,
add our voices to those who weep, sing, shout to you in
Arabic and Russian and Swahili
Korean and Serbian and Vietnamese
Spanish and Indonesian and Greek
Cantonese and German and Yoruba.

Make of our third world, second world, and first world
one world bound together by the gospel of Christ.
Let all the world in every corner sing your praise
until the sounds of our great thanksgiving
echo throughout the lands:
Gracias!
Danke!
Shukran!
Merci!
Thanks be to God who makes us one!

Praise

Creator God,
even the rocks cry out to praise you.
The trees clap their hands,
and the hills sing for joy.

In creation's chorus,
listen for our voice.
Hear our simple song
and note our parts.
We bring the sounds of our hearts,
noise like sounding gongs or clashing cymbals
and joy like a wren's melodic song.

Underneath our soul's music,
hear the echoes of pain we feel when another hurts,
the gasps of wonder at your creation,
the crescendo of our irrepressible gratitude for your gifts,
the gentle whispers of your spirit expressing
our feelings too deep for words.

We blend our voices with those of others
to create harmony we hope will be
acceptable in your sight.
With the rocks, the trees, the mountains,
the stars, the birds,
we sing in a chorus beyond "alleluia"
in the name of the one
who gives us a song to sing:

Praise, O praise, O praise the Lord!

Presence

God, through our fragmentary prayers
and our silent, heart-hidden sighs,
wordlessly,
your spirit bears our profoundest needs.

Deeper than the pulse's beat
is your spirit's speech,
making our human prayers complete
through prayer that is your own.

Let our jabberings give way
to the wordless hummings in our souls
as we offer our lives to you, our God,
whose presence makes us whole.

Reconciliation

Lord, you came looking for us and called us to follow. You asked us to serve, for there are too many hurts and too few healers.

But we were afraid that in touching the wounds of others we might meet and confront our own pain, and their nightmares would become ours.
. . . Lord, forgive us.

Lord, you call us to hear the sounds of pain others ignore, for in this world there are too many who cry and too few comforters.

But we were so busy protecting ourselves, we could not hear the cries of people abused in our streets and the whispers of love from those trying to make a difference.
. . . Lord, forgive us.

Lord, you call us to see the big picture, for in this world there are many who die slowly and too few who mourn.

But we were not ready to admit that millions of the world's children are victims of ethnic violence that costs them their childhoods, even, perhaps, their lives.
. . . Lord, forgive us.

Lord, you call us to speak against injustice, for in this world there are too many who live at the expense of others and too few who recognize that freedom is a gift.

But we were not ready to overturn the tables of power and status and become weak so that those now living in poverty might be strong.
. . . Lord, forgive us.

Lord, you call us to community, for in this world there are too many who imagine barriers of race, religion, economics, and age, and too few who imagine bridges blending language, tradition, and faith.

But we were not ready to transform our lives of isolation into walking symbols of peace.
. . . Lord, forgive us.

Lord, you gave us the earth to call our home, but in this world there are too many who are denied a cultural identity and a country to call their own and too few who fight on behalf of the oppressed.

But we have forgotten that freedom costs and matters, and have neglected our power to speak out for those who have no voice.
. . . Lord, forgive us.

Renew us. Call us again.

Send us out in unity with each other that we might take seriously the meaning of your requirement that we should do justice and love kindness and walk humbly with you, our God.

Revelation

"The word of the Lord was rare in those days,
and there were no frequent visions."

We cover our ears.
We hide our eyes.
We fall back asleep.
How will we know God's word for today?

In the middle of the night
and in the brightness of the day,
be attentive
to the voices that call your name.

Can we ever catch a glimpse
of the immortal, invisible God?
How will we begin to know
the One who is hidden from our eyes?

The Word has become flesh
and dwells among you,
full of grace and truth.

Let us seek the continuing revelation
of the God who speaks to us
in creation,
in silence,
in words,
and in Jesus Christ our Lord.

Seeking

God of all times and places, we move into this new year as travelers
seeking the shelter of your presence in all our comings and goings.
Like the magi we move from familiar surroundings, crossing borders
to enter unknown times and places.

**But we study maps and guidebooks, not stars. We are guided by
calendars and agendas, not faithful attention to the signs of your
presence. Transform the foreign geography of our lives into a land
of promise.**

Guide our hearts as we sort through our possessions for the things
we will carry on our trips. Enlarge our tents. May we welcome guests
with your hospitality, offering a place for them to tell stories or to
rest their voices and their souls.

**Make of our homes a sanctuary. Acquaint us with the pain of those
who seek refuge, a safe place from harm. Remind us that your children do not have to be physically homeless to be without a home.**

Extend our tables. Multiply our invitations. Guide us to persons
who need to share a meal rather than eat alone.

**Move us into the landscape of your world. Change us from
observers of ancient scenes to lively participants in the drama of
today.**

Remind us that the Word is not confined to an address, a country,
or a government but came to live where we live, full of grace and
truth and humanity and hospitality.

**Assure us that we do not travel alone. Guide us through stretches
of desert to the oasis of your love. Shine your Light on our path,
showing us the way to those who sit in darkness.**

Help us carry the memory of home, dropping it like bread crumbs
in the laps of those along our journey, so that they, and we, may find
our way back to you, our eternal home.

Water

Christ, you are like a mountain spring,
a fountain of living water.

**You are like a summer rain,
a sudden benediction.**

You are an ocean of calm
underneath our raging storms.

**You are like a waterfall,
an oasis in our desert.**

You are the source of our heart's survival
in the press of life.

**You are a cleansing flood,
a river of reconciliation,
washing away our sins.**

You are a bottomless well
of life-giving water,
full to overflowing,
drenching our souls
and quenching our thirsting spirits
with your peace.

**Praise to you, O Christ,
the Living Water of spirit and truth.**

Winter

God, we are prone to equate winter days
with barrenness and desolation.
When we do, we are just as likely to believe
you are as far away as the colors of fall and spring.
We confess that we slam doors
and lock windows and brood alone.

But into the darkness you place a star of light.
Into a world that still knows its Herods,
you place men and women
who pack up their dreams safely in their
hearts and head home a different way.

May we be among them, faithful against all odds,
setting out for who-knows-where.
Help us not be deterred by fatigue or rejection.
Let us not consider ourselves too powerful
or too wealthy to enter the homes
of those who know too much of winter cold.
Let us love the many faces of your world
and not be afraid of the strange and new.

At every turn we are blessed by your ancient love
continually and insistently sustaining us.
Through your Word, give us strength
to continue our winter pilgrimage,
searching for your Light to guide the way.

Wonder

The world is full of the grandeur of God.
Every fragrance, beauty, shape, texture, and color
reveals the imagination of our Creator.
So dig deeply into the world.

Lose yourself in the fiery brushstrokes of a sunset.
Pay attention to a starfish, a caterpillar, a petal, a feather, a pebble.

Let your eyes linger on the unfurling clouds.
Notice the way sunlight traces glory through the trees.

Celebrate a sliver of a luminescent moon in a blue-black sky.
Roll the smoothness of a stone over and over in your hands.

Step barefoot into the edge of a chilly winter stream.
Marvel at each peach, pear, plum, and pepper.

Soak in the first drops of an afternoon rain.
Stand stunned beneath the shifting shadow of an eclipse.

Give thanks for each daffodil, apricot, herb, or oak.
Turn over a rock to see what's hidden beneath.

Look through the lens of your soul at a single square foot of earth.
Wonder over the artistry of a Painting Bunting's feathers.

See that the Lord is good! Nothing is common.
Boundless wonder is everywhere.

Pay attention! For you may see the infinite wonder of our God.

Lent

From ashes to "hosannas" we follow you.
Walk with us through the desert, Lord,
even as we stumble and fall on our journey to the cross.
Create a holy pause in our cluttered lives.
Empty us of all that would keep us from
entering into your suffering for the sake of the world.

Brokenness

God, it takes courage to be the creatures
you made us to be.

Year after year we add to our experiences of the world,
pushing against our limits
to find out what will budge and what will not.

We find that we can make certain things happen,
and we can prevent other things from happening.
We can make friends, and we can make enemies.
We can say "yes," and we can say "no."

God, we confess that we get so carried away
that we begin to think we are in control of our lives—
until something happens.

God, we are tentative before you,
confused in the clutter of our abandoned dreams
and tattered faith,
worn out by our efforts to improve the world,
cramped by responsibilities,
and lost in an ocean of time.

In our brokenness we turn to you.
Resurrect the shattered pieces
into a stronger whole.
Take the fragments of our faith,
and in your mercy, Lord,
redeem them and make us whole.

Commitment

Create in each of us
a kneeling place,
where we may empty ourselves
of our self-importance
and become vulnerable
to your Word to us.

Help us set our faces firmly
against friendly suggestions
for safe, expedient lives.
and toward the risk of discipleship.
Loosen our grip on certainties
that smother possibilities.
Forgive our resistance to change.

Let us pursue the adventure
of losing our lives
in order to find them in you.
Guide us to follow
the way of the cross
where despair is transformed
by the promise of new life
and where we are compelled
to intercede for those
who have more pain in their lives than hope.

When we are too eager to be "better than" . . .
when we are too rushed to care . . .
when we are too tired to bother . . .
when we are too preoccupied to listen . . .
when we are too quick to act
from motives other than compassion
transform us,
hold our feet in the fire of your Lenten grace,
so we can see our actions
in the light of your costly love.

Communion

Welcoming God,
we give thanks that we can gather at your Table
as a whole fellowship,
a *koinonia* community,
not a mismatch of isolated believers.

If we were to talk with those breaking bread with us,
we might be surprised by everything
brought to the Table . . .
anticipation,
forgotten dreams,
splendid people,
hurting hearts,
unresolved questions,
memories of nourishing meals,
hard decisions,
desires to walk with you,
holding back.

The list is long, O God.
But somewhere in the midst of it
Christ is walking,
holding hands,
lifting up,
mending wounds,
breathing new life,
breaking bread,
pouring wine.

In remembrance of him,
we eat the bread of life
and drink the cup of the new covenant.
This is the heart of the gospel.
Thanks be to God!

Compassion

God, who loves the world so much,
we come to meet you here,
knowing not only that we are loved by you
but also that we have so much love to give away.

Help us decide what to do with this precious gift.
We can hold it tightly instead of loving other people.
We can clutch your steadfast love to ourselves,
or we can open our hands to see where your love will take us.

That's risky, God.
It may take us places we do not want to go;
it may call for confidence and strength we do not think we have.

O, God, sometimes it hurts to care,
to extend ourselves, to let other lives matter.
But God, when we really care, we can do nothing less
than listen with the ears of our hearts,
sit by a stranger who becomes a friend,
spend hours by a hospital bed.

When we do, we discover parts of ourselves
we left in the attic for years,
and we are pursued by the love of Jesus Christ who
came into the world and hurt with us,
cried over Jerusalem,
wept for Lazarus,
feels each pain,
suffers with
and loves every soul as if it were his only child.

O, God, we have much to repent
about the times we have not loved
and so much love to give away
because you have lavished love upon us.

Confession

For failing to renew ourselves through quiet withdrawal from a life of haste and confusion; for thinking that the journey you intend is always active and outward . . .

We confess our sins, O God.

For leaving it up to you to do the healing and caring work that we should be doing . . .

We confess our sins, O God.

For ignoring others when we are alienated from them rather than engaging in the difficult process of reconciliation . . .

We confess our sins, O God.

For failing to see your image in all things and in all people, even in ourselves . . .

We confess our sins, O God.

For straying so far from the truth that we find truth hard to recognize . . .

We confess our sins, O God.

For walking away from your invitation to be wholly ourselves before you and walking toward passions and pleasures that have become our gods . . .

We confess our sins, O God.

Cross

God, we are beginning a journey with you to the cross.
The word is almost too big.
We can't get our arms around it.
Its meaning staggers us.

But we hear you calling.
We see you motioning us to follow,
and we want to fall in step beside you.

When we are exhausted, raise us to walk again.
When we stumble, help us up.
When we want to turn back, keep encouraging us.

Grant us patience to smooth the way
for the advent of your reign.
Grant us hope that we may not be weary
in working for your peace for all people.

May we take seriously the meaning of your cross,
as we take up ours,
standing beside each other,
daring one another to take the risks you ask
so that together we can live out your mission in the world.

Discipleship

Gentle Shepherd,
some days we are as firm in our faith
as the disciples at their surest hour,
and sometimes we are like lost sheep.

Even when we are uncertain where the flock is going,
we believe you are ahead of us.
No matter how far we wander,
no one will snatch us from your hand.

Be patient with us, God.
Sometimes we panic easily. So calm us.
We refuse to be pushed. Gently lead us.
We make a lot of decisions based on our appetites.
Help us hunger for the things
that will truly nourish our bodies and spirits.
We may even butt heads for no reason at all.
Help us to be patient with each other.
After all, we are part of a flock.

You can see that we desperately need you
to be our shepherd.
We are depending on you to distinguish
the pain of one of us from the cry of another.
You know us each by name.

Teach us to listen to your distinctive voice
so that we may follow you.
and actually love one another as you have taught us.
For the tone of your voice is gentle.
Its words are strong; its meaning is love.
Will it be the only voice we follow?
This is our prayer.

Extravagance

Extravagant God,
who gave all,
even your life,
without calculating the cost,
your love is everywhere.

You do not hold your love back
to be admired from a distance
but pour your precious gift
out for us at great price.
Like perfume
from an overturned bottle,
it spills from your heart into ours.

So may we love—
purely,
dangerously,
wildly,
extravagantly,
creating a scandal of grace.

Let us love for love's sake,
seeing each day as the chance
to do a spontaneous,
irrational,
risky act of love
in Christ's name
whose love so amazing, so divine,
demands our souls, our lives, our all.

Forgiveness

God, hear our confessions . . .
for our running away from your love
to avoid the tug of your call:
. . . **Forgive us, God.**

for preferring the safe, familiar, and certain
to the risky, unknown, and mysterious:
. . . **Forgive us, God.**

for failing to believe in the vulnerability of power
and the power of vulnerability:
. . . **Forgive us, God.**

for taking no delight in variety
and insisting on sameness and conformity:
. . . **Forgive us, God.**

for fearing those different from ourselves
and projecting onto them what we cannot accept in ourselves:
. . . **Forgive us, God.**

for not noticing your presence in faces as well as in spirit,
in feeling as in intellect,
in darkness as in light,
in pain as in healing,
in the journey as in the resurrection:
. . . **Forgive us, God.**

Set us free, we pray, Liberating Christ,
so we may live our lives graciously and without fear.

Gospel

We believe in the gospel of Jesus Christ,
who comes to free the captives, heal the sick,
and proclaim the good news of the kingdom of God.

**We believe in a continually creating God
who calls us to costly love.**

We believe in a continually caring Christ
whose example encourages us to risk ourselves
for the sake of the gospel.

**We believe in a continually healing Holy Spirit
whose power enables us to share one another's burdens.**

We believe in a continually caring community called the church,
which is the physical presence of Christ in the world.

**We believe in a continually redeeming gospel
that brings wholeness and healing to each child of God.**

We believe in continually committing our lives
to freedom and justice and healing,
sharing our belief that the God who created us calls us still.

**We believe in continually participating in Christ's mission
to live out the gospel in the world.**

Hosanna!

How do we know you, Lord?

We know you through the power of your gentleness.

We know you are like a hen who gathers her chicks under her wing.

**We know you because you have pursued us with an undying love
that turns us from our fear and frustration
toward the life and light for which we were created.**

We know you because we have friends and family
who are with us when we feel like waving palms
and in times of deepest sadness when loss seems overwhelming.

We know you because you have assured us our prayers are heard.

Now we see you entering the holy city,
being worshiped as a king.
We find ourselves in the crowd, asking,
"Who is this before whom we sing 'glory, laud, and honor' "?

**Christ, our King, a ruler made known in brokenness and strength,
not in earthly power.**

Who is this before whom we wave our palms in worship?

**Christ, our Redeemer, who at the heart of the passion and pain
gives life in all its fullness.**

Who is this whose name brings salvation and life wherever preached?

**Christ, our Saviour, who lifts our hearts in praise: "Hosanna!
Blessed are you who comes in the name of the Lord!"**

Mystery

God, thank you for faithful signs
of spring that tell us you love the world.

Give us glimpses of your creation
that are sights for sore eyes—
a comet speeding through the sky,
green buds pushing their way onto bare branches,
your divine song echoed
by birds, streams, and rushing winds.
We human beings wonder at all you create
and rejoice to be a part of the living world
that you love and sustain.

We come in amazement, God.
The thought that you love us
even more than these glorious creations
is mystery indeed.

Open our ears to the sound of your voice
that resounds from the Creating Word,
the Holy Word that is behind every word,
the Mysterious Word that is you, our God.

god,
under
r of your wing.

often our nest
with comfort and care.
With vulnerable love,
you place yourself between
the source of pain and
your precious children.

Like a Mother Hen,
you try to shield us from suffering.
When we push against
your protection to move
into the world,
you give us life and breath and blessing.
You await and welcome our return.

Birth us again in your tender love.
Embrace us with your gentle spirit.
Cradle us in your presence.
Sing us the lullaby of your grace.

Openness

O, God of openness,
O, God of secret places,
we know the mistakes we have made.
We know how everything
can be going along fine on the outside
and then our wrongs are revealed
and nothing is right.

You know what we hide from you
and from others.
You know what we have done
and what we have forgotten to do.
You know how we have hurt others,
and in so doing, how we have
hurt ourselves and you.

O, God, forgive us.
Cleanse us through tears and prayer.
May we reach out to accept your grace in Jesus Christ.
May we be instruments of your love and grace and healing.
May we be truthful and ever in harmony with your purposes.
May we identify with our sisters and brothers in need
and stand by them,
no matter how much harder their lives may be than ours.
Give them grace and hope for the living of these days.

For all who are hurting inside,
for all who love so much,
for all who need your compassion,
for all who need forgiveness and need to forgive,
for all of us . . .
we ask your presence.
Walk with us.
Give us strength to finish the journey with you.

Pain

Out of the depths we cry:
"Where are you, God?"

Our pain is overtaking us.
Fear is crowding out hope.
Tears are flowing from a place
too deep for words.

Numbed by anxiety,
paralyzed by confusion,
we wrestle with what we believe.
We even refuse to be comforted.

Still, the bruises on our hearts
cry for love's healing.
We ache for you to enter our suffering.

Give us one small mercy,
so we will know you are with us.
Ease us into the healing of our pain.

Paradox

God of wholeness and healing,
we come to you
with our only plea being
that you accept us
as the paradox of people we are—
alone together
strangely familiar
diligently at ease
wholly scattered
extravagantly ordinary
anxiously hopeful
simply complicated
clearly mysterious
strongly fragile

That's who we are, God—
a little bit of this and a little bit of that.

In your mercy, Lord,
you see the whole of us,
not one part of us,
and still you call your creation good.
For your compassion,
we are grateful beyond words.

Bring us together in the
wholeness of your Spirit.
Heal us with your love.

Possibility

Fractured people we once were—cracked, broken, dried by the winds of the desert. Come, Lord Jesus! Deliver us again from the parched places.

Yours are the tears of the Spirit that weep with us.

A church we have become—born in wind and fire, not to be swept heavenward in a blaze of glory but to walk beside you down the dusty roads of this world. Come, Lord Jesus! Show us our God in skin and bones!

Yours is the breath of the Spirit that brought us together.

A resurrected people we will be—joyful, exuberant, risen, confident that your resurrection will restore what once was dead and is now alive. Come, Lord Jesus! Move our feet lightly to the rhythm of your song.

Yours is the movement of the Spirit that will dance with us.

Only you can turn our death into life, our mourning into dancing, our depths of sorrow into wellsprings of joy.

Come, Lord Jesus! Breathe your resurrection Spirit into us once again!

Renewal

Renewing God,
in this season called Lent,
our souls, like our surroundings,
need spring cleaning.

Shake us out so we can work
and walk with energy.
Blow off the dust and polish us
until we have the luster of your new creations.
Strip us back to the bare essentials.
Reach far into the corners of our lives
to pull out things we've left too long untouched.
Rub the windows of our souls
until others can see your reflection in them.

Help us make hard decisions
about what to keep and what to give away.
Let us know when enough is enough,
when we have all we can say grace over
and when we have space to care for more.
And as we pay attention to what is important,
let us make room for the new thing you
are preparing for us.

Dust.
Shine.
Polish.
Clean.

Renew our lives
until they are ready to receive
the fresh spirit of your spring.

Selfishness

God, forgive us
for being asleep
when you need us.

You agonize over the world's hungry
while we worry over the menu.

You weep with the soul
of one who is friendless
while we wonder
whom to invite to dinner.

God, forgive us
for neglecting your children
and not risking our security for their needs.

We know Christ's teachings.
We know the needs of the world.
We know ourselves.

God, forgive us for not transforming
what we have been taught
into what we do.

Trust

God of morning and evening,
God of sunshine and rain,
you possess all the rhythms of our lives.

In the evening you are the cradle of the world,
and in the morning you are our comforter.
You are here when we go away,
and you are waiting when we return.
You are the source from which our tears run unguarded
and the place from which our holy laughter rises.
You are the Creator, Redeemer, and Sustainer of our faith.

We claim that faith this morning,
convinced that it is real,
not by the persuasion of our minds
but by the stories our lives are writing.

We believe, O God,
but sometimes our days are fragile.
Our language is composed of sighs because there are no words.
Our vision is blurred because we do not know
what the week will bring.

Even when our faith is strong,
we feel the pain of others,
and it reminds us that we do not move through life alone.

For, lo, you are with us always,
even to the end of the age.

Waiting

Look upon us gently, Lord,
for waiting is not our forte.

So many other things are . . .
things like moving ahead,
fixing what's wrong,
planning what's next,
diagnosing the problem,
cramming more into a day
than one person can possibly do
before the sun goes down.

But waiting . . . .
when we are waiting for the light to shine,
when we are waiting for the Word,
when we are waiting for a wound to heal,
nothing in all the world
is harder than waiting.

So, in your mercy, Lord,
wait with us.
Be our very present help in waiting.
Heal our frenzy.
Calm our fears.
Comfort those who at this very minute
are with every anxious breath and thought
waiting for they know-not-what.

Transform our in-the-meantime
into your time,
while we wait with each other,
sit with each other,
pray each other into hope,
surrounded by your presence,
even in the darkness.
Especially in the darkness.

Easter

Risen Christ,
all creation sings with wild, exuberant hope.
In Easter joy and celebration
we echo the resurrection chorus:
"Christ is risen!
Christ is risen indeed!"
Alleluia!

Alleluia

Alleluia! Christ is risen.

Christ is risen indeed!

This is the Easter festival of life.
Let us celebrate the birth of the new,
the genesis of our re-creation in Jesus Christ.

**All creatures rejoice
in the powerful work of God's salvation.**

In Christ's resurrection hope triumphs over despair.

Alleluia to the Living Christ!

Love triumphs over hate.

Alleluia to the Living Christ!

Good triumphs over evil.

Alleluia to the Living Christ!

Belief triumphs over doubt.

Alleluia to the Living Christ!

Life triumphs over death.

Alleluia to the Living Christ!

Glory and honor and praise to Christ
who lives and reigns among us!

Alleluia to the Living Christ!

Christ is risen!

Christ is risen indeed!

Assurance

We celebrate good news:
Jesus Christ is risen!

God is our strength and our song;
God is our salvation.

When we lock ourselves away
in the upper rooms of our lives,
Christ's presence comes to us
with words of peace . . .

**words that send us out of our hiding places
with strength and power.**

When believing does not come easily
and we are more skeptical than faithful,
Christ's presence comes to us
with words of assurance . . .

**words that transform our anxiety to comfort
and turn our mourning into joyful dance.**

When tears cloud our eyes,
so we cannot see signs of resurrection,
Christ's presence comes to us
with words of hope . . .

**words that remind us of new life all around us
—even within us.**

Our assurance is in Jesus Christ,
Our Risen Lord.
Christ is risen!

Christ is risen indeed!

Belief

We believe in God,
who in love has shared the earth with all people.

**We believe in Jesus Christ,
whose resurrection gives us freedom and life.**

We believe in the Spirit of God,
who works in and through all who seek God's will.

**We believe in the community of faith
that is called to serve all people.**

We believe that in times of famine,
God's people plead for food;
in war, God's people demand peace.

**We believe that God overcomes the power of sin
and will establish justice and peace for all.**

But do we believe we can do what God asks?
We who have not seen villages of the earth's hungry—
can we be peacemakers nonetheless?

**Do we really believe that one letter,
one loaf of bread,
one life
can make a difference?**

**Our Lord and our God,
hear our prayer.**

Celebration

We celebrate you, Risen Christ.
We join every creature in proclaiming that you are worthy
to receive glory and honor and power forever and ever.

We celebrate you, Risen Christ,
for children who worship you through their wonder
in your world's sights and sounds and movements.

We celebrate you, Risen Christ,
for youth who seek your presence in the beauty of creation
and your compassion in the voices of others.

We celebrate you, Risen Christ,
for women and men whose lives are psalms of praise
tuned to glorify your name through their words and work.

We celebrate you, Risen Christ,
for congregations who fill their lives with faith,
their voices with song,
their hands with offerings,
and their words with gratitude.

We celebrate you, Risen Christ,
for the life of Jesus Christ
who was in the beginning, lived among us,
and now reigns forevermore as our resurrected Lord.

Companions

Divine Companion,
we should recognize you by now.
We've followed you down countless roads,
watching you with keen attention.
How can you be a stranger to us?

Risen Lord, open our eyes to you again.
Burn your truth into our hearts.
Be friendship's host and guest.
Stay with us until your resurrected presence
is blessed, broken like bread,
and placed in our hands.
Startle us with the cost of your friendship
that laid down its life for our sakes.

Because you called us "friends,"
let us live into that name
with our unending devotion,
our deepest listening,
and our genuine trust.

Envelop whatever
blessing, mending,
caring, healing,
welcoming, weaving,
reconciling
acts of love we can offer
our earthly companions
within the loving legacy
of your divine friendship.

Courage

God who created all things,
even the extravagant idea of resurrection,
we anticipate what is not yet
and practice your future
sometimes slowly, tediously,
always hopefully.

When we have anxiously looked at the sky this week,
we have been reminded
that a sudden summer storm can wipe the things
of this earth off their firm foundations.

We wonder what we would do if
we had to rebuild from the ground up.
Would we have the energy?
Would we have the spirit?
Would we have the vision?
Would our feet rest on the solid rock
of your love and grace and hope?
Could we be open to
the resurrection moments after Good Fridays?

You are our God, our Rock, and our Salvation;
Jesus Christ, the sure foundation of the church;
and the Holy Spirit, giver of gifts.
Make us co-creators with you,
so we may become more than we once were.

We offer our gifts to fit the geography
of the land before us—
a land of hope and promise,
filled with resurrection.

Mission

"Feed my sheep," you say.
Lord, these words don't give us any room for
wiggling out of your commandment.
If we are to be your sheepfeeding followers,
then we are signing on for costly love.
How can you really expect us to love as you love?

Yet in the echo of your words to Peter
we hear our own names before the haunting question:
"Do you love me?"
It reminds us that the measure of our love for you,
our shepherd, is our regard for your flock.

So in humble response, here we are, Lord, such as we are,
ready to tend your sheep as
listeners,
helpers,
hand-holders,
creators,
neighbors,
healers in your name.

Loved as we are, now let us love as
visitors to the sick,
givers of compassion,
blessers of children,
advocates for youth,
comforters of the crying,
makers of peace,
feeders of the hungry,
workers for a new world,
friends of the rejected,
speakers for those who have no voice.

Blessed as we are, now let us bless,
in the name of Christ, who is the face of costly love.

Music

Hymngiver God,

A psalm of praise we write for you,
O God of New Life,
who creates music in us we cannot contain.

A psalm of delight we write for you,
O God of Welcoming Presence,
whose hospitality invites us to linger at the table.

A psalm of gratitude we write for you,
O God of Transforming Promise,
who shapes miracles from words of hope.

A psalm of rejoicing we write for you,
O God of Eternal Love,
who embraces us in the circle
of creation, redemption, and resurrection.

Composer of Wonder,
make of us living psalms of praise.

Proclamation

The Lord be with you.

And with your Spirit.

Lift up your hearts.

We lift them up to the Lord.

Let us say what we believe:

**We find our faith in Jesus,
who lives among us,
who calls us together to understand
life and love as radical commitment to others.**

**We have faith in one God,
who created and claimed all creatures,
who enters our lives with hope and
redemption and courage to act on our beliefs.**

**We know that God's presence
comes to us in community,
wherever we seek to know God
by doing justice and loving mercy.**

**Once we were no people,
but now we are God's people.
Once we had not received mercy,
but now we have received mercy.**

**Because all things are possible through God's love,
we proclaim the gospel in this world
where God is still creating and redeeming
and making things whole.**

Promise

Designer and Sustainer of Life,
you are with us in welcome breezes of hope
and parables of love
acted out in the daily dramas of our lives.
You are with us in the gifts that create life,
bless it, and keep it.
In all these signs of resurrection,
we hope and pray that we recognize your presence.

We also know you are with us in the Good Fridays,
days that do not only come marked on a calendar
but whenever suffering and pain
swallow us or someone we love.
You are with us
when the foundation crumbles,
when we are scared or shattered or sad,
and we pray without urging
if not without ceasing.

Remind us that you are not the source of pain
but you are with us in the pain.
You are where love is.

God, we claim your loving presence
for those who are anxious or fearful today.
Be their Gentle Healer.
Collect their tears in your hands.
Let them feel your presence beside them,
steadying their hearts until they breathe as one with you.
Give us strength to let go of all that holds us back
from entering the sufferings of others.

Remind us that nothing in all creation
will be able to separate us from
the love of Christ Jesus our Lord.

Resurrection

When others dismiss your story as an idle tale,
who will you be?

Resurrection people with Easter in our hearts.

When the world seems to be crumbling around you,
remember who you are:

Resurrection people with Easter in our hearts.

When despair would seem to squelch all hope,
believe in who you have become:

Resurrection people with Easter in our hearts.

When it is hard to persevere against all odds,
trust in God who names you:

Resurrection people with Easter in our hearts.

As we follow Christ into the world,
may God help us remember who we are . . .
resurrection people with Easter in our hearts.

Seasons

Everlasting God,
when summer days are long,
we move from early daylight to late sunsets,
noticing the gifts of the season:
fresh vegetables ready to be picked in the cool of the morning,
trees offering a pool of shade on a hot afternoon,
glittering light of fireflies at night.

All these gifts refresh us, God,
and remind us that your love for us
knows no special season.
Guide our eyes to holy moments
we might otherwise miss.
Unfold our gifts with the gentle power
of a blossom opening petal by petal.

Turn our eyes in hope toward you,
our God of all creation,
all nurturing love,
and all new life.

Through the seasons of our souls,
we join with all nature in manifold witness
to your great faithfulness, mercy, and love.

Surprise

Surprising God, keep us expectant, open, sensitive, alive.

When we expect a desert, give us cool rain.
Give us music when we expect trouble.
When we expect anger, give us calm.
Give us silence when we expect noise.

When we expect loneliness, give us memories.
Give us sleep when we expect restlessness.
When we expect questions, give us prayers.
Give us hopefulness when we expect helplessness.

When we expect emptiness, give us tears.
Give us sisters and brothers when we expect friends.
When we expect bread and wine, give us Christ.
Give us strength when we expect exhaustion.

When we expect comfort, give us challenge.
Give us a feast when we expect a meal.
When we expect fairness, give us justice.
Give us community when we expect a crowd.

When we expect religion, give us a spirited church.
Give us flashes of your glory when we expect commonplace.
When we expect death, give us resurrection.
Give us extravagance when we expect enough.

Surprise us with your overwhelming grace.

Table

Christ, our Host,
Christ, our Guest,
what better place to meet you than at the Table.

Every time we pass the bread and the cup
to each other in this community,
we know your hands are guiding ours.
Since early on the morning of creation,
you have been planning this meal,
kneading the bread with your strong and gentle hands,
setting a place for each of us,
sending out the invitations.

And now we are here, accepting your welcome.
You are our Host.
But we realize that you are also our Guest,
who has come to dine with us.

What a privilege it is to offer
our ordinary food and drink to you,
knowing that when you touch it,
it will not be just bread,
not just a cup of wine.
When we eat and drink together in your name,
our meal is more than a meal.

We hold in our hands the bread and the cup
that bind us in holy communion
to believers everywhere today
and to all who have gone before us.

May we remember once more the gift of your life
and our calling to set the table
for those who have no bread.

Witness

God of Creation,
creating anew,
the silence is broken.

With the women in the garden
we catch our breath,
wipe our tears,
and try to articulate our
experience with you.

What words can describe
shadows fleeing from the tomb?
How can we tell of the morning
the world turned upside-down?
No mortal words will do.

Still, we must spread the news:
Christ is risen!

Our knees are weak from running;
our voices tremble
on the edge of fearful joy.
Our eyes have seen the glory
of the Lord loosed upon the world!

May every breath we take,
every word we utter,
everything we do,
witness to the truth
of Christ's resurrection.

Pentecost

Spirit of God,
Wind of God,
Fire of God,
make known your presence, your work, your justice,
and your love real to the world through us.
Here we are, your church on mission,
your hands and feet in the world.
Set our hearts on fire.

Abundance

God of the hungry,
Shelter of the homeless,
Provider of all we need
and much of what we want,
you welcome us
like a parent calling a child
to a nourishing meal.

Coming together as one family
reminds us that both our affluence
and our want are known to you,
our fullness and the things
for which we starve.

As you replenish us with
food for our souls,
turn our eyes and hearts
to the needs of our brothers and sisters
who go to bed hungry
and wake up longing for bread.
Help us realize how much is enough
and how much is too much
to hold lightly in our lives.

Give us enough trust
to live secure in your love
and to share it freely with others
in open-handed confidence
that your grace,
like loaves and fishes,
will never run out.

Advocacy

Let us come before God with our prayers,
trusting in a God of love and hope,
of justice and forgiveness.
God who cares for children, hear our prayer.

For all children,
especially those who are neglected or left behind,
help them receive the nurturing they need.
God who cares for children, hear our prayer.

For all youths,
especially those who live on the edge of fear,
help them find an accepting place to grow.
God who cares for children, hear our prayer.

For all parents and grandparents,
especially those who struggle to provide for children
in the midst of poverty, violence, and racism,
help them find strength in you and support in community.
God who cares for children, hear our prayer.

For all congregations,
especially those that minister in a society of affluence,
help them find their true meaning in you.
God who cares for children, hear our prayer.

For ourselves,
especially when we lose sight of the children in our midst,
help us celebrate them and care for those
who do not have anyone to delight in their presence.
God of all children, hear our prayer.

Always

God of now and then and in between,
we give our deepest thanks
that you are the God of our hearts
and the God of our history.

You promised to be with us always,
even to the end of time.
Remind us that your "always" is
past, present, and future.

But, Lord, even knowing that, we confess
that "in the meantime" living is not easy for us,
for today some of us are especially fragile.
Some of us are remembering moments
that changed the path of our spiritual lives.
Some of us are sorting out feelings,
trying to make sense of a bigger picture.
Some of us are wondering how we can reach out
to those who are hurting deeply.
Some of us are longing for the past
or wishing that the future would come quickly.

O God, we knew your faithfulness yesterday.
Assure us of your presence today.
Remind us of your steadying power
when the ground underneath us is shaking.
Especially when we are teetering on the edge of changes,
help us take the time we need
to keep the balance only your presence can give.

Sustain us through the living of these days.

Beginning

God of all things old,
God of all things new,
we invoke your presence
on the edge of this new week.

Some of us are as comfortable with being here
as we are in cushiony, well-worn shoes.
Some of us feel as though
we are in new clothes with the creases still in them,
wondering if we give clues
that our confident outward appearance
defies our inner anxieties.

Others come like second graders,
secure with familiar routines
yet standing on tiptoe,
eager to see what will be different this year.
Some of us are like teenagers,
ready to see friends above all else,
knowing the work before us is worth the effort
but too much to tackle alone.

In-the-beginning God,
however we come to you—
nervous or scared,
excited or rested,
hopeful or blessed,
or a mixture of all of these—
we seek your blessing this morning
as a prelude to the week ahead.
Continue the good work you have started.
Help us not only to realize
that you have begun a good work in us,
but that you call us to completion
in the grace and name of Jesus Christ our Lord.

Bread

Nourishing God,
you ate bread with friends
and multiplied it for five thousand people.
You described your kingdom as yeast.
You claimed for yourself the identity of bread.
You gave your body to be broken for the world.

Often we eat our meals
without smelling the aroma of fresh loaves leaving the oven.
We buy flour to make our bread,
but seldom walk the land that produced the grain,
while many in the world still gather raw grains each day.
They plant, pick, and grind their harvest
and shape the dough into tortillas,
chapatis, loaves, pitas, rolls.
They feel the flour, the meal,
or the corn between their fingers,
literally touching their daily bread.

Bread of Life,
give us a taste of tender bread from your table.
Move the deepest parts of our spirits to compassion
for our brothers and sisters
throughout this whole wide earth
who are praying for rain for their crops,
buying and cooking only what their family needs for today,
and waiting for the nourishment that will sustain them.
We are bound to them in our humanity
and in our hunger for you.
Break our hearts as bread for the world.

Change

Everlasting God,
you are the source of our common life.

You bring us together; you send us apart;
and you bring us together again.
You are faithful to us when we seek your presence.
You are faithful to us when we don't know which way
to turn in our wandering.
You are faithful to us when we are nonchalant
in our attention to you.

Often we get things just like we want them,
and something happens that throws everything
into a different light forevermore.

In the lean times and in the abundant times,
remind us that all time is your time.
In this time of change,
help us recognize what is essential
to our common life as a community of faith.
Your voice is our map.
We know that we live in the secure hand
of your promise for a redemptive future.

But sometimes, when we cannot see the road ahead,
it's hard to trust your promise.
As we travel together,
help us recover our identity as your people.

May we listen carefully when we hear our calling:
"Live now."
"You are the church."
"You are on mission with me."
"You need each other."
"Christ needs your hands and feet in the world."

God, empower us for the future
with all we need to be the church today.

Children

God our Mother, God our Father,
thank you for children,
signs of the kingdom
growing by leaps and bounds among us.

With unconditional love,
may we gather them into our circle.
Let us tell them your story
again and again and again
until they imagine it, paint it, sing it,
act it, dance it, write it—
until it sinks deep into
their bodies and spirits and voices,
until they express their joy and sadness
from head to toe.
Remind us that children come
"trailing clouds of glory,"
not so far from the wonder of your face.

Forgive us for watering down the gospel
until you are just another grown-up
who "went about doing good" long before they were born.
Forgive us for telling them to be kind and loving
without offering them the faith and hope they need
to live authentically in the world.

Even as we try to shelter them from storms,
help us model compassion that enters the pain of others.
Let us nurture all that makes them precious gifts,
daughters and sons made in the image of God.

Above all, as we grow alongside our children,
may our dependability and faithfulness
show them they can trust your tender love
now and forever.

Church

Young and old,
sons and daughters of God,
all you who are the diverse creations
of God's imagination and love,
join in praise and thanksgiving
as we worship the One
who brings us together.

**We come to this place,
bringing our varied stories,
our unique gifts,
and our distinct calls to serve.**

We come together in partnership and mission,
knowing that we are called to be the church:
to celebrate God's presence,
to serve others,
to seek justice,
to offer the hope of the Resurrected Christ.

**We are called to be the body of Christ—
a community of believers,
a household of faith,
a communion of saints,
the people of the covenant.**

We are called to the one hope of our high calling—
one Lord, one faith, one baptism, one God.

**As members of the body of Christ,
we covenant together in this hour
to build on our sure foundation of Jesus Christ our Lord
and to seek the vision of Christ's hope for the world.**

Comfort

Spirit of Christ,
You are our comforter,
our helper,
our advocate,
our very present help in times of trouble.

You do not leave us alone.
Your faithfulness is not an accident,
and our faith is not born of chance.
We test you at every turn,
and you are still there.
We wonder if we will get through the hard times,
and by your grace we do.
We worry about strength for tomorrow,
and then we remember your faithfulness yesterday.

Spirit of Christ,
enter our hearts with your peace
that passes all understanding.
Come quietly into hospital rooms,
and wait with us.
Come gently into homes where there are tears,
and catch them in your hands.
Come calmly into our anxious schedules,
and give us awareness of your presence.

In our human ways,
may we be for others
comforters,
helpers,
advocates,
people who help in times of trouble,
always in the Spirit of Christ,
our Comfort beyond all comfort.

Community

God of our community and the whole community of believers,
it is right and good that we pause in the middle of Pentecost
to think about the way your Spirit moves among us.

God, we thank you for the community of faith with which we pray:
for the differences among us by which we are enriched
and through which the Spirit prompts us to grow;
your amazing grace that forgives and restores us;
new insights from ancient, holy words;
traditions of the church that still give us meaning today;
hymns and prayers that pour out of our hearts into yours;
Christian friends who perceive our strengths when we cannot;
words of encouragement, affection, and trust;
shared laughter, healing of wounds,
and hope shining as a light in the darkness.
For all these things, we give you our deepest gratitude.

We wonder how we can reach out to those with whom we pray
who are struggling with pain we cannot comprehend.
We wonder how we can make a difference in a hungry world.
We wonder how we will meet the demands of this week.
Give us the strength we need to be your church,
to accept the cost and joy of discipleship,
to be gracious in the service of others,
to proclaim the gospel to all the world.

When our call seems overwhelming, teach us the value of
one hand extended in love,
one word expressed in care,
one plate of food for a hungry person,
one moment of rest in a day of work,
one voice of hope lifting a lonely spirit.

Take all these gifts we offer; add your blessing.
Receive them as our worship during the week.
Use them for the sake of your mission in the world.

Creativity

Creator God,
everything around us reflects your majesty:
the wind that bends the trees,
the creatures that fill the air and land,
the great planets and stars that light up summer nights.
Wherever we turn,
we see your divine splendor.

But it was only upon the hearts of women and men
that you imprinted your image.

So we, your children,
have fashioned reflections of you
with our creative gifts:
art and architecture,
music and literature,
poetry and photographs,
steeples and crosses,
banners and children's drawings,
Bach fugues and carefully tended gardens,
and food lovingly prepared.

These are our offerings to each other
in your name—
our unique ways of saying
you are here among us.

Let us create new songs of praise to you, our God.
Let us discover fresh ways of proclaiming
your greatness and glory.

Dreams

Remember waking up with a dream
that held you in its power?
We remember hearing the voice of God
whispering into our ears
and the hand of God resting on our shoulders.

Did you believe your dream could come true?
Or did you dismiss your dream as wishful thinking?
We believed in our dreams with all our hearts.
But we were younger then,
and no dream was too outlandish
or too extravagant for us to chase.

Treasure the dreams God sent you. Let them shape your life.
We will not lose confidence in our dreams.
We will dream a dream that belongs to all of us,
not to any one of us alone:

where your sons and your daughters shall prophesy,
your old men shall dream dreams,
and your young men shall see visions;
where your old women shall wake with hope in their eyes,
your women shall catch their joy,
and your children shall imagine more than you ever dreamed:

a world where their daytime dreams are blessed
and their nightmares are no more;
a world where the blind shall see, the deaf shall hear,
and the lame shall dance;
a world where people are not judged by the color of their skin;
a world where all God's children feast at the welcome table;

a world where we no longer see in a mirror dimly but face-to-face
with Jesus Christ, who dares us to dream God's dream.

We remember the dream Gold sent us—
a dream of justice and healing and love.
Let us hold fast to the vision of our Dream-Giver God.

Encouragement

Loving God,
how good it is to know persons
who give us reason to call you
Loving God,
Caring Parent,
Accepting Friend,
Comforting Companion.

Sometimes we like to imagine
we are independent sorts.
And then we remember
mother,
father,
grandparents,
brothers,
sisters,
friends,
children,
teachers,
mentors,
one person,
another,
yet others,
a "cloud of witnesses," our own cheering section,
who through your grace saw something in us
we didn't see in ourselves,
who helped us discover the gifts in our hands.

So many have given us so much.
So many have cared unconditionally.
Lord, hear our gratitude for the people
who have shaped our lives and been there all along,
who have helped bring us this far by faith.
For our splendid, devoted friends and family,
our encouragers, we give you deepest thanks.

Faithfulness

God of this morning,
God of every morning,
you are God enough for all of life.

When it's summertime in our souls,
we may forget to thank you
for the high and holy moments.
But when we are weak or scared or sad,
we call out for your help without thinking twice.

This week has reminded us that life is not easy,
that it costs and matters.

Carry our prayers to those
who need the continued promise
that you are the God of hope and wholeness,
who rises in resurrection
above all that could lead to despair.

For even in all the gray and sadness of life,
your love will not let us go.
With your persistent love, remind us that
in the ocean depths of our lostness,
you are there.
In the moments of resurrection,
you are there.
In the depths of our gratitude,
you are there.
In the heights of our anxieties,
you are there.

Make the night as bright as the day,
the seas calm, the rough places plain.
Fold your joy into all the pain and loss.

Break us, as morning, into reflections
of your faithful love.

Friendship

God, if anything makes us rich, it is our friends.
We could offer a litany of names of those we call "friend"
in the truest sense of the word,
people who let us be fully ourselves.
With them we feel relaxed, comfortable, at home.
In the mystery of your spirit, our souls find kinship.

We move through risky places, hard questions,
even ordinary days, knowing our friends walk with us
and taste the salt from our tears.
Our stories connect in strange and wonderful ways,
creating a common history.

Today, God, we bring our friends to you in prayer:
younger friends who call us to life and wonder,
who open the places in our souls we closed long ago;
older friends who mentor for us the vision of experience
and see treasures in us we do not see in ourselves;
friends of our own generation who share common memories.

God, hear our prayers for our friends:
for our friends who are risking what is safe and familiar—
we offer the security of our care.
For our friends facing times so difficult they wonder
if they will ever breathe easily again,
not worrying about tomorrow—
we offer our hearts beating as one with theirs.
For our friends who are separated from us by the distance
of geography or spirit—
we offer the vulnerability of our love.

God, in Jesus Christ you showed us
the ultimate model of friendship.
By your grace, we pass your gift to others.

Grace

Faithful and loving God,
we bring our fragmented lives
into the presence of your wholeness.

We bring our wandering thoughts
into your eternal light.
We bring our restless spirits
into the calming strength of your grace.

We give you thanks
because even in moments of great anxiety,
when the threads of our lives are hanging loose,
chaotic and disconnected,
we can be confident that you are with us.

We're too busy to stop,
hurling ourselves through life,
weary from holding up a big section of the sky.
We confess . . . and we confess again . . .
we have labored under the assumption
that the way to find rest for our souls
is to finish our list of things to do
and present it to you like a book.
Forgive our compulsiveness.
We forget that your grace envelops us.

Oh, God, remind us that we do not have to go it alone.
When we look down the road
we see Jesus,
waiting to heave the weight of our load
onto his shoulders.

In your mercy, Lord, we claim your grace.

Gratitude

For these gifts and more, we give thanks to God.
patches of sunlight, kindred spirits, hope for the future,
a good night's sleep, creativity, wide open spaces, healing,
God's presence from everlasting to everlasting,

the good kind of tired after a job well done, safe returns,
strength to walk and not be weary, grandparents, redbud trees,
rivers, lakes, and ponds, the preciousness of life, hugs,
uncles, silent nights, playgrounds, smooth stones and seashells,

church suppers, bread that is more than bread, faithful friends,
psalms, hot chocolate, purple pansies, candlelight, teachers,
good neighbors, faith to live into our callings, shooting stars,
storm homes, memories, parents, youth who keep us seeking,

nativity scenes, sons, courage to risk, peace like a river,
relationships that deepen through the years, walks in the rain,
starry skies, good books and movies and conversations,
chili on a cold night, hymnwriters and poets, vegetable gardens,

friends who catch our tears, aunts, ministering together,
invitations, people who live out the gospel, smiling eyes,
comfort and joy, maps, autumn leaves, holy moments, mentors,
forgiveness, language that is in words and beyond words,

rice for the hungry, sitting at the table together, blowing kisses,
doctors' and nurses' healing hands, daughters, solitude,
expectancy, overflow of gratitude, wind of God's spirit,
mission trips, babysitters, hummingbirds, caretakers, picnics,

birthday parties, finding what was lost, shoulders to lean on,
wonders of God's love, resurrection, children's drawings,
adagios and crescendos, those who tug us toward justice,
strength for today and bright hope for tomorrow,

Streams of mercy, never ceasing call for songs of loudest praise.
For these gifts and more, we give thanks to God.

Hands

God, whose hand moved across the
face of the deep and created all things,
accept the gifts of our hands.
Like Moses, we are amazed
that what we hold in our hands
is holy and acceptable in your sight.

For, God, you know how much we need
hands that lift us up,
hands that clap in joy,
hands that tend gardens,
hands that turn pages in books,
hands rough from doing justice,
hands wrinkled after years of caring,
hands that have not pulled back from the bedside of pain.

O, Lord, let us beware of being alone,
of folding our hands
or curling our fingers toward ourselves.
For you are the Creator of relationships,
the Blesser of friendships.
You called us into community,
so we may be your hands and feet in this world.

Remind us that no hand is
too small,
too scarred,
too manicured,
too rough,
too clumsy
to hand a gift to another.

No hand is too slow, too quick, too sure
to pass your peace to a sister or brother in Christ,
whose hands were wounded for our sakes
and touch us with blessing even now.

Healing

God of healing,
we bring our prayers to you.
Our prayers at this moment →
are not those we prayed yesterday,
nor not are they the ones
we will pray tomorrow.
For we are a little farther along
than we were yesterday,
and we are not where
we will be tomorrow.
Some of us are a bit stronger;
some, a little more fragile.

In our strongest moments
and in our weakest ones,
your Spirit heals us
in ways we do not understand.
Remind the sad and lonely
you do not despise a broken heart
but welcome its tears.
Remind the fearful ones
that fragile people shall yet dream dreams.
Remind those aching for others
that one day the lame shall leap for joy,
the blind shall see, and the deaf shall hear.

What can we believe, O God? *This we believe, O God*
— That the touch of your mercy
will ease our pain →   *and give us the courage*
that and your spirit will help us care, one for *one another* *to grieve.*
that the strength of your healing comes
in the midst of our deepest heartaches,
in our shimmering joys,   *and crushing sorrows*
and in our crushing sorrows.
God, whose steadfastness outshines the sun,
we lean on your steady love.
                healing

107

Heritage

This is the day the Lord has made.
Let us give thanks:

for our ancestors in the faith
who have made this day
of gathering with God's people a reality,

for our brothers and sisters in the faith
who walk beside us
to help find the possibilities of faith today,

for our ancestors in the faith
who passed on the treasures of God's word
in the form of ancient scrolls,

for our sisters and brothers in the faith
who translate words of Holy Scripture
into modern texts of words and deeds,

for our ancestors in the faith
whose experience in God's providential care
moved them toward trust in God's steadfast love,

for our sisters and brothers in the faith
who are journeying with us
toward your new mercies every morning,

for our ancestors in the faith
who began telling the story of God's extravagant love
for us through Jesus Christ,

for our sisters and brothers in the faith
who listen to us tell of the hope and joy
we know in Christ who lives among us.

Let us live as stewards of both past and promise,
blessing the ancient story
and celebrating the new day of our life together.

Holiness

We sing of you, our Holy God,
who is immortal and invisible;
our God who is light inaccessible hid from our eyes.
You are unresting, unhasting, and silent as light.

In you, Eternal God,
we encounter mysteries we cannot comprehend;
the majesty of your ways far surpasses our richest imagining.

We long for a thousand tongues to sing
the praise of you who calms our fears;
your name sings its own music in our ears.

In you, Gentle Shepherd, we see God on Earth;
we know the tenderness of your embrace
and the compassion of your care.

We sing of you, our God,
who leads us beside still waters
to restore our souls and quiet our restless hearts.

In you, Great Redeemer,
we see the blind receive their sight,
the lame jump for joy, and the broken-hearted rejoice.

But sometimes our best worship of you is silence.
Still our bodies; still our voices; still our souls
so that we may enter your presence in holy silence.

May this be our true worship.

Hospitality

God, you are here when we arrive,
and you are here when we leave.
You move with us into new places,
and you give us glimpses of the home
for which we are looking.
You call out our names
as though each of us were
the one lost child
for whom you were searching.
Your face lights up
when you see us coming into your presence.

You welcome us when we arrive
on the doorstep of your home,
looking for a place
to feel safe and secure from all alarms.
You prepare an extravagant table for us,
setting it with food that nourishes our body
and company that feeds our souls.
You give us a word to carry with us
into days that might seem longer and harder
without the assurance that you are going with us.
You are our home.

Now God we want to prepare a home for you.
We are looking for you.
Hear us calling your name to be with us.
Watch our faces light up
when we recognize your presence.

Dine with us.
Talk with us.
Sit in silence with us.
Be at home with us,
in the name of Jesus Christ,
who came to live among us.

Hunger

God of the South African child and the North Korean child,
God of the Bangladeshi woman, the Nicaraguan man,
the wandering refugee, and the grandmother in the projects,
God of every last one of us,
we come linked by our places in this world
where the sun laps time zones from today into tomorrow.
We are connected as family members on this earth
who have the power to bring to the Table
bread and fish, rice and noodles,
oranges and potatoes, corn and beans, so everyone can eat.

But, God, we confess that in a world where there is food
enough for everyone, we squander our power
to distribute the food on our shelves
or the money in our pockets to the hungry.

We admit that we come to this day
looking for an easier answer than sacrifice.
We know that the awareness of injustice
we feel at this moment
may fade as quickly as today's headlines.

So, God, give us compassion that lasts.
May we give whatever is within our power
to overturn the tables of injustice
and to pour out bags of rice
for all those the world forgets to feed.

Trusting in your power,
we join with your people everywhere
who long for the day when we will never have to calendar
a "World Hunger Sunday" again,
when all the grain is distributed,
when every parent's hungry child is fed,
when justice and joy prevail.

Inclusivity

God of all peoples of the earth,
we gather in your presence,
aware of the vastness of your world
and the intimacy of your concern.

We pray for our society,
populated by billions of people
and filled with thick newspapers
full of words that speak too much
about division.

We pray for the smaller world around us,
for the members of our families,
for friends who share our concerns,
for those who depend on us and on whom we depend.

Keep teaching us that your circle is always
larger than our perceptions,
for we are tempted to get cozy with
a few in the living room and ignore
the closed doors of our souls.

We want to repent of our small vision,
to break out of all that confines us
on our right and on our left.
Transform us to live by your expansive vision.
Stand us foursquare in the midst of all
that is broken and hurting in our world.
Direct our eyes beyond the visible to see
your kingdom breaking into our lives.

Let us transform gospel words into action,
living out the truth that Christ has
broken down the dividing walls of all
that would hinder our being united in his name.

Justice

Disturbing God,

When we forget that you created each person in your image,
shock us into the reality of your justice for all people.

When we impose our own will over those already oppressed,
shock us into the reality of your justice for all people.

When we increase the volume of self-serving speech
while others have no voice,
shock us into the reality of your justice for all people.

When we are silent in the presence of enemies of peace,
shock us into the reality of your justice for all people.

When we fail to make room for the needs of others
in our familiar places,
shock us into the reality of your justice for all people.

When we turn our backs on the pain of others rather than walk
with them toward their healing,
shock us into the reality of your justice for all people.

Disturb us with your unguarded compassion
until justice rolls down like waters
and righteousness like an everflowing stream.

Mercy

Bless the Lord, O my soul; and all that is within me,
bless God's holy name!

**You have given good gifts to us, your children.
You have entrusted us to share your blessing
with generations yet to come.**

The Lord is merciful and gracious,
slow to anger and abounding in steadfast love.

**Sometimes we have journeyed into far countries,
spending our gifts in foolish ways;
we have wronged each other and sinned against you.**

God does not deal with us according to our sins,
nor requite us according to our iniquities.

**Instead, God's amazing response is to wait for us with open arms,
ready to clothe us in mercy and grace.**

As far as the east is from the west,
so far does God remove our transgressions from us.

**God puts robes on our tired backs, rings on our busy fingers,
and sandals on our dusty feet.**

The steadfast love of the Lord is from everlasting
to everlasting upon those who fear the Lord.

**For in Christ the dead live again; the lost are found.
This is cause for rejoicing. Let the celebration begin!**

Ministry

As members of the body of Christ,
we wonder at God's imagination that designs a gifted community.
What gifts has God given you?

Listening
Peacemaking

Hospitality
Teaching

Caring for the earth
Seeking justice

Humor
Organizing

Compassion
Communication

Music
Encouragement

Creativity
Remembering

Some of us are gifted to comfort and nurture.
Some of us call out gifts in each other.

Some of us understand the needs of children.
Some of us advocate for youth and the elderly.

God's mission in the world is carried out
wherever God's people offer their gifts for ministry.

**We are the body of Christ and individually members in it.
In bringing our gifts together
we recognize our dependence on each other.
We offer our gifts through this church,
knowing we can do more together
than we could ever do apart.**

Power

Almighty and loving God,
you created the ocean depths;
you made the mountains rise;
you spangled the sky with stars.

We praise your majestic power
revealed in all creation.

When the earth trembles
and our hearts shake with fear,
we look for a steady place to stand.
That's when we yearn for your gentle power
to come to us, in ways that
speak comfort and peace
to our very human hearts.
In the midst of all that changes,
we look for a love that endures.

So God, pour your holy power
on each one here
in ways that reveal
your quiet strength,
your hopeful presence,
your faithful love.

Rest

When we are carrying heavy loads,
O God, who never wearies, give us rest.

When we are exhausted from a hard day's work,
O God, who never wearies, give us rest.

When we feel the stress of too much to think about,
O God, who never wearies, give us rest.

When we grieve for ourselves or for others,
O God, who never wearies, give us rest.

When we think we can't go on,
O God, who never wearies, give us rest.

When we feel tired from being alone,
O God, who never wearies, give us rest.

When we feel far away from you,
O God, who never wearies, give us rest.

When we feel guilty about a wrong we have done,
O God, who never wearies, give us rest.

When we are treated unjustly,
O God, who never wearies, give us rest.

When we are heavy with hopelessness,
O God, who never wearies, give us rest.

Silence

God, it feels rude to break the silence,
short as it was.
We had hardly begun to be quiet,
and now we are back into words.

In our search for you,
we confess that we
reflect too much,
analyze too much,
talk too much,
figuring out,
thinking aloud.

God, give us more silent space,
so we can discover the world
beyond our making.

Be the Word that comes
to dwell in the silence,
authoring sentences of calm,
paragraphs of comfort.

And help us always remember
that in silence we can know indeed
that you are God.

Simplicity

Loving God,
do we make your message too hard?
We worry that if we don't
study enough,
interpret enough,
struggle enough,
wrestle enough with the words
we won't understand what you really want us to hear.

But when we are resting in your presence,
we realize that your purpose is not to make life
a puzzle for us, complex and confusing.
You know we need plain and simple messages:
"Love God with all your heart."
"Love one another."
You give us the simple gifts of
sabbath rest,
poetry and music,
hands to hold,
and comforting words.

But sometimes we want to make you all mystery
and forget to look for the mystery of you in the ordinary.
When we hold out our hands, give us ordinary bread,
and through it remind us of the extraordinary gift of
your body broken for us.
When we hold the cup, give us ordinary wine,
and through it remind us of the extraordinary gift of
your blood poured out for us.

Through them both,
through all of life,
may your simple words be the most profound ones we hear:
"God is love."
"God is love."
"God is love."

Spirit

Come, believers and faithful ones,
sing your "alleluias" to God!

Praise God,
who invades us with the rush of a mighty wind
and fills us with fire.

Praise God,
who out of love for all humanity
sent Jesus Christ to live among us.

Praise God,
whose Spirit is poured out upon all flesh
so that our sons and daughters might prophesy.

Praise God,
whose Spirit is not hindered by the barriers of this world
but moves freely to offer community and hope.

Praise God,
who empowers us with gifts
and calls us each by name.

Come, Holy Spirit.
Dream dreams through us.
Imagine with us.

Breathe, oh breathe,
your loving Spirit into our world.

Stillness

Quietly,
we come to you in prayer.
During this hour we want to be still
and know that you are God.

So much of our existence is spent
in scrambling and searching
that we forget what quietness
and contemplation are.

Today we ask for a steadying,
a refocusing,
a reshaping,
of our lives.
Let us meet you
at the deepest places
of our hearts.

We know we cannot stay still.
We must move again.
But out of this time of stillness,
may we go steadier and surer
of who you are
and who we are.

May our breath
move in and out
as one with yours.

In the silence,
we rest,
we worship,
we open ourselves to you.

Tears

God, we seek your face
for we have known its smile,
its delight in our very presence.

We have known times of faith
that were like waking up
and, realizing that we're in your arms,
we sighed contentedly and continued our rest,
assured of our safe place with you.

We seek your face
because we have known its tears,
its pain over the suffering of the world,
its sadness over the hurt places in our hearts.
When we cry, we know that you taste
the salt from our tears.

Show us your tear-stained face
in the panorama of people
who have passed your story down to us
from generation to generation.
Show us the memory of your face
in the people who have been part of our own
flesh-and-blood faith stories.
Show us the vision of your face in the mosaic
of people we have yet to meet—
a picture of children and youth and adults
broken by a world that is mostly unpredictable,
who long for a loving, caring face that will never go away.

Through us, smile your grace upon them.
Wipe their tears.
Bless them and keep them.
Lift up your countenance upon them.
Make your face to shine upon them
and give them peace.

Thanksgiving

Generous and gracious God,
we give thanks for your gifts great and small:
Lord of all, to thee we raise, this our joyful hymn of praise.

For the beauty of the earth, for the glory of the skies,
the unspeakable beauty of the stars, smooth stones and seashells,
and the moment of slowing down before a peach and violet sunset:
Lord of all, to thee we raise, this our joyful hymn of praise.

For those who have joined our congregation,
the memory of those who are gone,
and relationships that deepen through the years:
Lord of all, to thee we raise, this our joyful hymn of praise.

For the good kind of tired after a job well done, the rhythmic
cadences of Sundays that call us together,
and those things yet possible:
Lord of all, to thee we raise, this our joyful hymn of praise.

For hymnwriters and poets who capture what we're feeling inside,
fragile openness after utter guardedness,
and language that is beyond words and in words:
Lord of all, to thee we raise, this our joyful hymn of praise.

For raising us to life in this time and place,
safe returns from important journeys,
and enough restlessness in our hearts to move faithfully with you:
Lord of all, to thee we raise, this our joyful hymn of praise.

Vocation

You have listened for the voice of God in sacred places, particularly within your own heart and soul and mind.

We have watched you increase in wisdom and in years and in divine and human favor. The delight we take in your presence in our lives is a reflection of God's joy over you.

Like the Hebrew Samuel, you awakened to a voice calling you in the night. You recognized the voice as God's and responded to God's call.

We believe the story of your call is an expression of God's continuous revelation in your life.

We rejoice that you have found the place where your deep gladness and the world's deep hunger meet. Therefore, we bless and affirm your ministry, whatever shape it may take.

May you continue to know God's healing even as you offer yourself as an instrument of God's healing to others.

May you be surprised by God's light in the darkness when you need the illumination of divine guidance.

May the passion you feel for your calling give wholeness and life to your vocation.

Above all, know that no matter where your call may lead you, our prayers will surround you, Christ's peace will go with you, and God's love will sustain you. This is our assurance and our hope.

Thanks be to God.

Wholeness

Spirit of God,
you are the source of renewal,
rebirth, and re-creation.

You focus on what is most broken;
all that looks like it is beyond repair.
With the breath of redemption,
you take the tiniest shards of hope
and restore them to more than they once were.
You do not shy away from horrific valleys,
stormy mountains, or dry plains
but move in where others fear to tread.

You came into the world as a God-with-skin-on,
who knows the things for which we thirst
and those that make us rise up and dance.
You instill us with breath
apart from which there can be no life.
Help us realize that we are mere mortals,
and all the wind we can huff and puff
into our most desperate situations
is not enough until we breathe as one with you.

Now breathe the wind of your spirit
through the soul of our church
until the doors rattle
and the foundations shake
with the movement of your power
and we know again that you are the Living God.

Make us vulnerable to the needs of a broken world.
Call us from nothingness to wholeness,
from death to life.
Let us listen for your call to rise up and live.

Spirit of God,
we wait breathlessly upon you.

Worship

Then Moses gathered the whole community and said, "Bring your offering to the Lord." And the people's hearts were stirred, and their spirits were moved. They looked for gifts to bring.

And they brought all kinds of gold jewelry—pins, earrings, rings, and necklaces. They brought wool and linen—blue, purple, and scarlet. Others brought silver and bronze, the finest wood, onyx stones, spices, oil, and fragrant incense.

Are these the same kinds of offerings you make to the Lord? **Centuries have transformed the shape of our gifts, but time has not changed the spirit of our offerings. Our hearts, too, are stirred by the generosity of the Lord; our spirits are moved by God's faithfulness to God's people.**

What offerings do you bring to present to God in worship? **We bring scores of music, chiming bells, guitars, trumpets, and violins. We offer voices young and old—singing voices, praying voices, reading voices, noisy voices. We give money that represents our work. We bring our silent wonder and faithful presence.**

What symbols of community do you bring? **We bring velvet banners that remind us of the church's celebrations, deep purple and blazing crimson and elegant turquoise. We offer gifts of fabric and wood, paint and clay. We give the work of our minds to teach our children and youth and write our stories. We bring our care for each other's needs.**

What symbols of our mission to the world do you bring? **We bring Holy Scripture that reminds us to live as sisters and brothers. We bring bread broken in remembrance of Christ who brings us together and then sends us out to serve. We give all your hopes and dreams to God's vision of a holy people.**

We are the church—**the community born of grace, the family blessed by Christ's Spirit, the holy people of God.**

Year

"O God, our help in ages past,
our hope for years to come . . ."

How often we have spoken and sung those words this year!
And now, here we are on the doorway of hope,
peering into Advent and the future,
looking back over our shoulders to see where we've been.
This one thing we know, God—
that wherever the months have taken us,
your hands have never let us go.

We come to you today in thanksgiving
for the constancy of your care.
You have moved with us through the seasons—
from the darkness of Advent to glimmers of light,
from the despair of our spirits to signs of resurrection,
from the bluster of winter winds to the flurry of summer activities,
from the breezes of spring to the rushing wind of Pentecost.

When we were full of questions and doubts,
you were with us in our confusion—and we give thanks.
When the ground on which we were living
began to shake like never before,
you were with us in our fear—and we give thanks.
When we didn't have a map for where the church was going,
you were with us in our dreams—and we give thanks.
With holy discernment, you have guided us
to the edge of the future.

Now may we grasp the hem of the new year
with faith born of all we have learned of you,

"O God, our help in ages past,
our hope for years to come."